W9-ANW-400

What Are Rules and Laws?

Ellen Ripley

PowerKiDS
press™

NEW YORK

Published in 2013 by The Rosen Publishing Group, Inc.
29 East 21st Street, New York, NY 10010

Book Design: Michael Harmon

Photo Credits: Cover Nelson Marques/Shutterstock.com; pp. 4, 19 Hemera/Thinkstock.com; p. 5 Hannahmariah/Shutterstock.com; p. 6 Stockbyte/
Thinkstock.com; p. 7 © iStockphoto.com/Blue_Cutler; p. 8 Thinkstock/Thinkstock.com; p. 9 Wavebreak Media/Thinkstock.com; p. 10 Fuse/Thinkstock.com;
p. 11 Jupiterimages/Thinkstock.com; p. 12 Onur ERSIN/Shutterstock.com; p. 13 Photo Researchers/Photo Researchers/Getty Images;
p. 14 Creatas/Thinkstock.com; p. 15 fotog/Getty Images; p. 16 Digital Vision./Thinkstock.com; p. 17 Stephen St. John/National Geographic/Getty Images;
p. 18 iStockphoto/Thinkstock.com; p. 21 Lisa F. Young/Shutterstock.com; p. 22 Dmitriy Shironosov/Shutterstock.com.

Library of Congress Cataloging-in-Publication Data

Ripley, Ellen.
What are rules and laws? / Ellen Ripley.
        p. cm. — (I'm an American citizen)
Includes index.
ISBN: 978-1-4488-8860-3 (pbk.)
6-pack ISBN: 978-1-4488-8861-0
ISBN: 978-1-4488-8585-5 (library binding)
1. Law—United States—Juvenile literature. 2. Legislation—United States—Juvenile literature. 3. Bill drafting—United
States—Juvenile literature. I. Title.
KF387.R57 2013
349.73—dc23

                                                2012013258

Manufactured in the United States of America

CPSIA Compliance Information: Batch #WS12RC: For further information contact Rosen Publishing, New York, New York at 1-800-237-9932.

Word Count: 514

Contents

What Are Rules?   4

Following the Rules   6

Laws   12

How Are Laws Made?   16

How a Bill Becomes a Law   20

Glossary   23

Index   24

What Are Rules?

Do you have to follow any rules? Your parents might give you rules at home. You have rules at school, too. You even have rules when you're playing a game.

Class Rules

Listen when someone else is speaking

Work quietly at your desk

Raise your hand when you need help

Treat others with respect

Play Safely - Make wise choices

Respect the personal property of others

There are a lot of rules we have to follow. Rules are important because they tell us what we can and can't do. Rules keep people safe and make things fair for everyone.

Following the Rules

Your parents may make a lot of rules. They tell you when to go to bed or when you can watch TV. Sometimes it's hard to follow the rules, but it's important.

Rules keep you from doing things that might hurt you.

They also keep you from doing things that are bad.

Rules keep you safe and help you grow up to be

a good person.

Teachers make rules at school, too. One rule is
that you have to raise your hand when you want to talk.
This shows that you **respect** your teacher and
the other students.

Teachers make rules to keep things fair. This means everyone has to act the same way. This is one way that rules help us to be happy.

We have rules when we play games and
when we play sports, too. Sometimes it seems
like there are a lot of rules, but we have
to learn them all.

Having rules for games and sports keeps everything fair.

It also helps the players stay safe and out of trouble.

Playing by the rules makes sure everyone has fun.

Laws

Did you know that our **government** has rules, too?

The rules the government makes are called laws.

Laws are rules that all **citizens** must follow.

Laws are like rules, but they're even more important.

You can get in trouble if you don't follow laws.

In the United States, our leaders make laws. Laws keep us safe and make sure we have order in our towns and in our country.

One law is that we must drive on the right side of the road. Everybody has to follow this law. If we don't, a lot of people could get hurt.

How Are Laws Made?

It takes a long time to make a law. First, government leaders listen to everyone's ideas. The people tell the leaders what should become a law.

Then, leaders write something called a bill.

A bill tells everyone why something should be a law.

The other leaders in **Congress** have to read the bill.

If the other leaders like the bill, they **vote** to pass it. This means that they say yes to it. More than half the leaders must say yes to pass a bill.

If the leaders pass the bill, it goes to the president.

The president reads the bill and decides if he likes it.

If he likes it, he signs the bill. Then it becomes a law.

How a Bill Becomes a Law

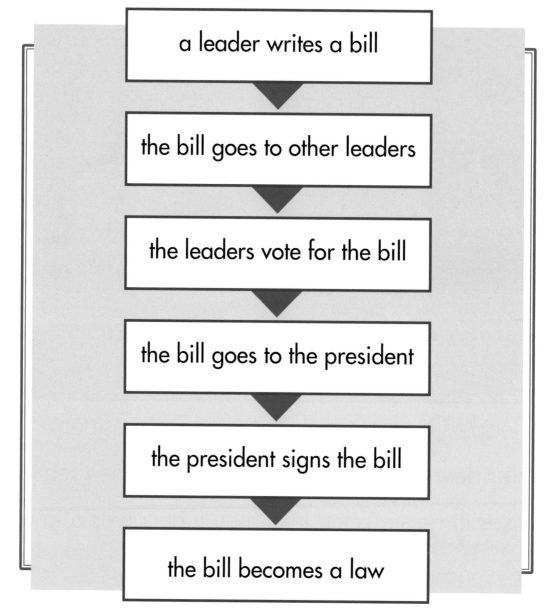

a leader writes a bill

↓

the bill goes to other leaders

↓

the leaders vote for the bill

↓

the bill goes to the president

↓

the president signs the bill

↓

the bill becomes a law

Some people have the job to make sure
that everyone follows the law. Police officers work
to keep our towns and cities safe.

Rules and laws help us stay safe and happy.

It's important for everyone to do what's right.

It shows others that you're a good citizen!

Glossary

citizen (SIH-tuh-zuhn) Someone who belongs to a country.

Congress (KAHN-gruhs) One part of the United States government.

government (GUH-vurhn-muhnt) A group of people who rule a country, state, or city.

respect (rih-SPEHKT) To feel or show special thought for someone or something.

vote (VOHT) To pick something.

Index

bill, 17, 18, 19, 20

citizen(s), 12, 22

Congress, 17

fair, 5, 9, 11

game(s), 4, 10, 11

government, 12, 16

leader(s), 14, 16, 17, 18, 19, 20

parents, 4, 6

police officers, 21

president, 19, 20

safe, 5, 7, 11, 14, 21, 22

school, 4, 8

sports, 10, 11

teacher(s), 8, 9

vote, 18, 20